Prudence Crandall
Teacher for Equal Rights

by Eileen Lucas
illustrations by Kimanne Smith

On My Own
BIOGRAPHY

Carolrhoda Books, Inc./Minneapolis

The photograph on page 46 appears with the permission of the Prudence Crandall Museum, Canterbury CT/CT Historical Commission.
The portrait of Prudence Crandall was painted by Carl Henry in 1881. It is a copy of a painting by Francis Alexander, done in 1834.

Carolrhoda Books, Inc.
A division of Lerner Publishing Group
241 First Avenue North
Minneapolis, Minnesota 55401 U.S.A.

Website address: www.lernerbooks.com

Library of Congress Cataloging-in-Publication Data

Lucas, Eileen.
    Prudence Crandall : Teacher for equality / by Eileen Lucas; illustrations by Kimanne Smith.
        p.   cm. — (On my own biography)
    ISBN: 1–57505–480–9 (lib. bdg. : alk. paper)
    1. Crandall, Prudence, 1803–1890—Juvenile literature. 2. Teachers—United States—Biography—Juvenile literature. 3. Quakers—United States—Biography—Juvenile literature. 4. Discrimination in education—Connecticut—History—19th Century—Juvenile literature. 5. Canterbury (Conn.)—Race relations—History—19th Century—Juvenile literature. [1. Crandall, Prudence, 1803–1890. 2. Teachers. 3. Quakers.] I. Smith, Kimanne, ill. II. Title. III. Series.
LA2317.C73 L83 2001
371.1'0092—dc21   00–010625

Manufactured in the United States of America
1 2 3 4 5 6 – JR – 06 05 04 03 02 01

Author's Note

This story begins in 1832. At that time, most black people in the United States lived in the South as slaves. Slaves were treated as if they were property. Slave-owners made their slaves work long hours. Many slaves did not have enough food to eat. They could not come and go as they pleased. In the North, where this story takes place, slavery was against the law. But blacks in the North did not have the same rights as white people. Some white people did not think that black children should be able to go to school with white children—or even have schools of their own. These people also believed that black people and white people should not eat together, live in the same part of town, or sit next to each other in church.

Other people believed this kind of thinking was wrong. Prudence Crandall, a white teacher and a Quaker, was one of them. Quakers were against war and prejudice. To the Quakers, a good education was very important. Prudence Crandall believed that everyone should be able to go to school. This is the story of her struggle to make education available to everyone.

November 1832

Prudence Crandall opened the gate
and stepped inside the yard.
She looked up at the Canterbury
Female Boarding School with pride.
She had opened this school one year ago.
Her students were girls from
Canterbury, Connecticut, and other towns.

Some students walked
to classes each day.
Others lived in rooms above the school
because their homes were far away.
Prudence taught the students
reading and geography.

She also taught
sewing and good manners.
The students' parents were pleased
with all that Prudence taught.
Some said that this school was
the best of its kind in the state.

One day, Prudence had a visitor.

Sarah Harris had been to

the school many times before.

She often visited her friend Mariah there.

Mariah worked for Prudence.

But this time,

Sarah had come to talk to Prudence.

When Sarah was younger,

she had gone to the local school.

In some New England towns,

young black and white children could

go to school together.

Older white children went to

white-only schools.

But there were few schools

for older black children.

Some of Sarah's white classmates had

become students at Prudence's school.

Sarah wanted to go to

Prudence's school, too.

She wanted to teach other

black children someday.

Prudence listened to Sarah.

But she did not give her

an answer right away.

She knew the townspeople expected

her to teach white students only.

For many weeks,

Prudence thought about what to do.

Prudence did not like it when

people were unfair to others

just because of the color of their skin.

Prudence was a Quaker.

Quakers believed in

honesty and fairness.

Prudence decided that she would

teach Sarah Harris.

January 1833

Prudence's decision made
people angry.
A group of parents
came to see Prudence.
They did not want a black girl
in school with their daughters.
They said that Sarah must
leave the school.
If she did not,
they would take their daughters home.
They told Prudence the school
would sink without students.
"Then it will sink," said Prudence.
"I will not turn her out."

Many students did leave the school.
Soon, the school might be
forced to close.
Prudence thought about
what she should do.

Refusing to teach
black students was not fair.
She decided she would close her school.
Prudence wanted to open a new school
for young black ladies.

Prudence went to Boston to see
a famous abolitionist
named William Lloyd Garrison.
Abolitionists believed
that slavery was wrong.
Many also believed that free black people
should be treated fairly.
William Lloyd Garrison
listened to Prudence.
He agreed to help her find black students
for her new school.
Prudence traveled to other cities to spread
the news about her new school.
Then she returned to Canterbury.
She told her white students
that the school was closing.
She told them about her new school.

The townspeople
were shocked by the news.
They called a town meeting.
Town leaders shouted that a school
for black girls would ruin Canterbury.

18

A minister from a nearby town
tried to speak up for Prudence.
His name was Reverend Samuel May.
The town leaders
would not listen to him.
They had made up their minds.
They would destroy the school.

19

April 1833

Prudence opened her new school in April.
Black students came from
Connecticut and other nearby states.
They were happy to have
a good school to go to.
The leaders of Canterbury did not
welcome the new students.
Storekeepers would not sell food
or supplies to the school.
The town doctor refused to help the
students when they were sick.
Even some churches
turned the girls away.
When the students went for walks,
boys blew horns in their faces.
Others threw stones and dirt at them.

But Prudence and her students
refused to give up.
Prudence found ways to get supplies.
A friend brought food
from a store in another town.
The girls found other churches
that welcomed them.

Prudence admired the girls
for their bravery.
The townspeople were
so cruel and full of hatred.
But the students
tried to ignore the insults.
They kept busy with
their studies.

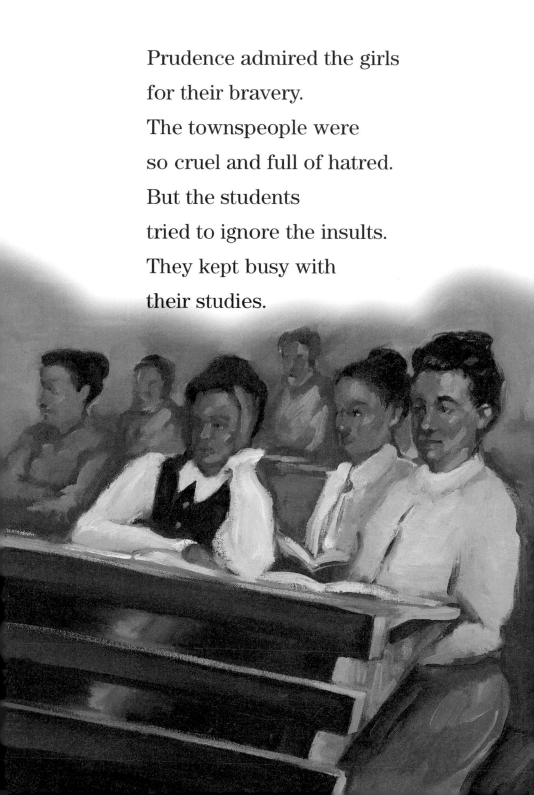

The people of Canterbury
still wanted the school closed.
They asked their
state leaders for help.
In May of 1833,
Connecticut passed the Black Law.
It stated that no school could accept
black students from other states
unless local people agreed.

The people of Canterbury celebrated.
They rang bells and fired a cannon.
They were sure that Prudence
would close her school now.
But they were wrong.
Prudence did not accept
the new law.

June 1833

One summer day, there was
a knock on the school door.
The sheriff had come
to arrest Prudence.
She had broken the Black Law.
She would have to pay a fine
called a bond.
Otherwise, she would go to jail.
Prudence wanted to show
that the law was wrong.
She refused to pay the bond.
That way, people would know how angry
she was about the Black Law.
Prudence rode with the sheriff
to the jail.

Reverend May asked Prudence
if she was afraid to go to jail.
"Oh no," said Prudence.
"I am only afraid they
will not put me in jail."
She remembered stories of Quakers
who suffered for what they believed in.
These thoughts made her brave.

"Clang!" went the door of the jail.
Prudence was locked in.
The next day, Reverend May
paid the bond.
Prudence returned to her school.
But she had broken the law.
She would have to go
to court in August.

The townspeople became
even more hateful.
They threw stones and rotten eggs
through the school windows.
Prudence moved the desks
away from the windows.

Then someone dumped garbage
into the school's well.
The students could not
drink the water.
Prudence's father brought
water to the school from his farm.

In August, Prudence's
trial date arrived.
The angry people of Canterbury
filled the courtroom.
But some of Prudence's
friends were there, too.
An abolitionist named Arthur Tappan
came from New York to help Prudence.
He paid for her lawyer.

The people of Canterbury said that the
school broke the laws of Connecticut.
Prudence's friends
said that the laws were unfair.
The court could not
decide who was right.
So Prudence had to have
a new trial in October.
This time the jury said that Prudence
was guilty of breaking the Black Law.
Prudence's lawyers asked
for another trial.
They wanted another chance to prove
that the law was wrong.
They met to prepare
their case for Prudence.

The townspeople continued
to fight the school.
On a cold January afternoon,
one of the students smelled
smoke in the schoolhouse.
Soon the whole house filled with smoke.
Someone cried, "Ring the fire bell!"

The people of Canterbury came
to put out the fire.
They did not like the school,
but they did not want
the town to burn down.
With some repairs, the school
would be safe again.

July 1834

A few months later,
Prudence was back on trial.
This time the judges did not say
if Prudence was right or wrong.
They didn't say that the Black Law
was unfair, either.
It was hard to know who won.

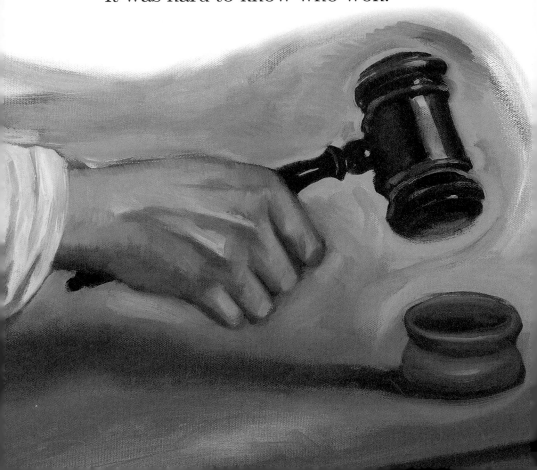

Prudence's lawyer explained
that her school could stay open.
Prudence was glad for her students.
But she wished the judges
had put an end to the Black Law.

During the trials, Prudence had met
a man named Calvin Philleo.
He was a Baptist minister
from New York.
Prudence and Calvin
liked each other right away.

When Calvin asked Prudence
to marry him, she said yes.
Prudence and Calvin were married
after her last trial.
With much to be done at the school,
there was no time for a wedding trip.
Prudence returned to teaching.

September 9, 1834

One night, Prudence and her students
woke to the sound of glass shattering.
Men with clubs and iron bars
were smashing many of
the school's windows.

Some men crawled through
the windows and broke furniture.
Nothing this bad had happened before.
Prudence was afraid that
next time they would hurt the girls.
She had had enough.

The next day, Prudence
decided to close the school.
Reverend May came to help.
He said, "I felt ashamed of
Canterbury, ashamed of Connecticut,
ashamed of my country."

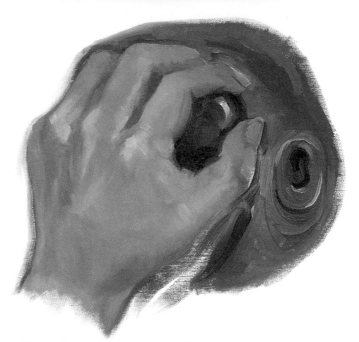

Prudence was sad.
But she was also proud.
She would always remember
the faces of her students.
She would remember how
happy they were to be in school.
As she closed the school door
for the last time, she knew
that opening the school
had been the right thing to do.

Prudence Crandall at age thirty

Afterword

Prudence Crandall sold the schoolhouse and moved with her husband to New York. In 1838, the Black Law was repealed, or canceled, in Connecticut. Many of the men who had passed it admitted that the law was unfair. Prudence moved back to Canterbury for a short while. She later settled in Kansas.

Prudence was one of the first teachers to fight for equal education for all. Because of her efforts, others were able to accomplish more later on. In 1867, Howard University, a school dedicated to the education of black youth, opened in Washington, D.C. Booker T. Washington, a former slave, founded the Tuskegee Institute for black students in 1881. Hearing about these accomplishments made Prudence proud.

Prudence died in 1890. Many of her former students carried on her work. Some, including Sarah Harris, became teachers who taught black students. Great strides had been made. Still, black students often had fewer and older books than white students. Teachers in black schools worked under difficult conditions. It wasn't until 1954 that the U.S. Supreme Court outlawed separate schools for black students and white students. By accepting Sarah Harris into her school, Prudence Crandall took one of the first steps toward equal education for all.

Important Dates

September 3, 1803—Prudence Crandall is born in Rhode Island.

November 1831—Prudence opens a school in Canterbury, Connecticut.

January 1833—Sarah Harris begins attending Prudence's school.

February 1833—Prudence announces that the school will close and reopen for black students only.

April 1833—The new school opens.

May 1833—Connecticut passes the Black Law.

June 1833—Prudence is arrested.

August 1833—Prudence stands for her first trial.

October 1833—The second trial takes place.

January 1834—A fire damages the boarding school.

July 1834—The third trial takes place. The judges dismiss Prudence's case.

August 1834—Prudence marries Calvin Philleo.

September 1834—Men attack the boarding school and cause severe damage. Prudence decides to close the school.

1838—The Black Law is repealed.

1886—Connecticut promises to pay Prudence a pension.

January 28, 1890—Prudence dies in Elk Falls, Kansas.

1969—Connecticut buys Prudence's former home and school and turns it into a museum and library for black history and women's history.